D0904751

Disasters for All Time

THE ATTACK ON PEARL HARBOR

KERSHAW COUNTY LIBRARY
632 W. DeKalb St. Suite 109
Camden SC 29020

WITHDRAWN

Valerie Bodden

CREATIVE EDUCATION • CREATIVE PAPERBACKS

Published by **Creative Education**
and **Creative Paperbacks**
P.O. Box 227, Mankato, Minnesota 56002

Creative Education and Creative Paperbacks
are imprints of **The Creative Company**
www.thecreativecompany.us

Design and production by **Joe Kahnke**
Art direction by **Rita Marshall**
Printed in China

Photographs by Alamy (Trinity Mirror/Mirrorpix, ZUMA Press, Inc.), Creative Commons Wikimedia
(Kaboldy, National Diet Library, Naval History and Heritage Command/80-G-71198, Naval History and
Heritage Command/C-5904, Petty Officer 2nd Class Diana Quinlan/DVIDS, US archives, Work permit),
Getty Images (Bettmann, Historical/Corbis Historical, Michael Ochs Archives/Moviepix, Ralph Morse/
The LIFE Picture Collection, Pool/Kyodo News, Roger Viollet), Library of Congress (LC-DIG-fsa-8a31173/
Library of Congress Prints and Photographs Division), LostandTaken.com, National Archives and Records
Administration (195617/Roosevelt, Franklin D./Franklin D. Roosevelt Library Public Domain Photographs;
520595/Department of Defense; 520600/Department of Defense; 520641/Department of Defense; 520746/
Department of Defense; 535795/Office for Emergency Management, Office of War Information, Overseas
Operations Branch, New York Office, News and Features Bureau; 537944/Department of the Interior,
War Relocation Authority/Lange, Dorothea, Photographer), National Museum of Naval Aviation
(NNAM.1996.488.029.040/Robert L. Lawson Photograph Collection, NNAM.1996.488.029.087/Robert L.
Lawson Photograph Collection), Shutterstock (Natasa Adzic, vadimmmus)

Copyright © 2019 Creative Education, Creative Paperbacks

International copyright reserved in all countries. No part of this book may
be reproduced in any form without written permission from the publisher.

Library of Congress Cataloging-in-Publication Data
Names: Bodden, Valerie, author. Title: The attack on Pearl Harbor / by Valerie Bodden.
Series: Disasters for all time. Includes index.

Summary: A historical account—including eyewitness quotes—of the devastating 1941 attack on the American
naval base at Pearl Harbor and its wartime aftershocks, ending with how the disaster is memorialized today.

Identifiers: LCCN 2017051379 / ISBN 978-1-64026-001-6 (hardcover)
/ ISBN 978-1-62832-546-1 (pbk) / ISBN 978-1-64000-020-9 (eBook)

Subjects: LCSH: Pearl Harbor (Hawaii), Attack on, 1941—Juvenile literature.

Classification: LCC D767.92.B597 2018 / DDC 940.54/26693—dc23

CCSS: RI.3.1-8; RI.4.1-5, 7; RI.5.1-3, 8; RI.6.1-2, 4, 7; RH.6-8.3-8

First Edition HC 9 8 7 6 5 4 3 2 1
First Edition PBK 9 8 7 6 5 4 3 2 1

CONTENTS

December 7, 1941, dawned bright and clear in Hawaii. Sailors at Pearl Harbor Naval Base enjoyed a slow morning. It was Sunday, so there was no need to rush. Some ate breakfast. Others dressed to visit Honolulu. None of them knew that danger lay only 230 miles (370 km) away. There, six Japanese aircraft carriers bobbed in the choppy waters of the Pacific Ocean. The ships carried more than 400 bombers and fighter planes. Japanese pilots prepared to attack. Their target was Pearl Harbor.

Just before 8:00 A.M., Japanese planes screamed over Pearl Harbor. They dropped bombs and torpedoes on the American ships below. The sky blackened with smoke. Sailors rushed to their battle stations. But they could do little to stop the attack. By the end of the day, more than 2,400 Americans were dead. Less than 24 hours later, the United States was at war.

I

WORLD AT WAR

The attack on Pearl Harbor came at a time when much
of the world was already at war. World War II had
begun in September 1939, when Germany invaded Po-
land. Italy and Japan soon formed an alliance with Germany. Together, the three countries became known as
the Axis powers. They were opposed by the Allies. The
Allied forces included Britain and France. They were
later joined by the Soviet Union.

People in the U.S. knew about the war in Europe.
Most did not want to get involved in it. Only 20 years
earlier, the U.S. had fought in World War I. More than
100,000 American soldiers had died. In addition, many
Americans worried about problems closer to home. The
Great Depression had left many people without jobs
or homes. Some struggled to buy food.

In 1940, France fell to German forces. After that, the

German forces, led by Adolf Hitler's Nazi Party, gathered at annual rallies such as this one at Nuremberg in 1936.

The war enabled many American women to work outside the home and take jobs as welders, assemblers, and mechanics.

"Modern war ... is too tragic and too devastating to be approached from anything but a purely American standpoint. We should never enter a war unless it is absolutely essential to the future welfare of our nation.... America has little to gain by taking part in another European war.... Our safety does not lie in fighting European wars."

- Charles Lindbergh, American aviator and "America First" proponent, 1939

U.S. provided weapons and other supplies to the Allies. The U.S. also began to build up its army and navy. But it did not send any troops to the war. A German submarine torpedoed an American **destroyer** in the fall of 1941. But still the U.S. did not declare war.

Many in the U.S. military worried more about Japan than Europe. Japan was a small island nation with few natural resources. It depended on the U.S. and other countries for oil, coal, and rubber. Japan wanted to end its reliance on the West. Japanese leaders planned to do this by taking over

Japan's invasion of China began the Sino-Japanese War, which lasted from 1937 to 1945.

resource-rich countries in Southeast Asia. In 1937, Japan invaded China. By 1941, Japanese troops had reached Vietnam, Cambodia, and Laos. In response to the invasion, U.S. president Franklin Roosevelt banned the sale of American oil and metal to Japan. The U.S. also bulked up its naval fleet. It moved part of the fleet to Pearl Harbor. This naval base was located on the Hawaiian island of Oahu.

Some American leaders saw Pearl Harbor as a perfect base. Coral reefs protected the shallow harbor. Two mountain ranges ringed the island. Other military officials saw Pearl Harbor as a trap. The harbor had a narrow entrance. Ships had to enter and exit single-file. They could not make a quick launch. In addition, the naval base often ran short on ammunition, spare parts, and fuel. These supplies had to travel 2,400 miles (3,862 km) from the U.S. mainland. Supply ships needed several days to reach the base.

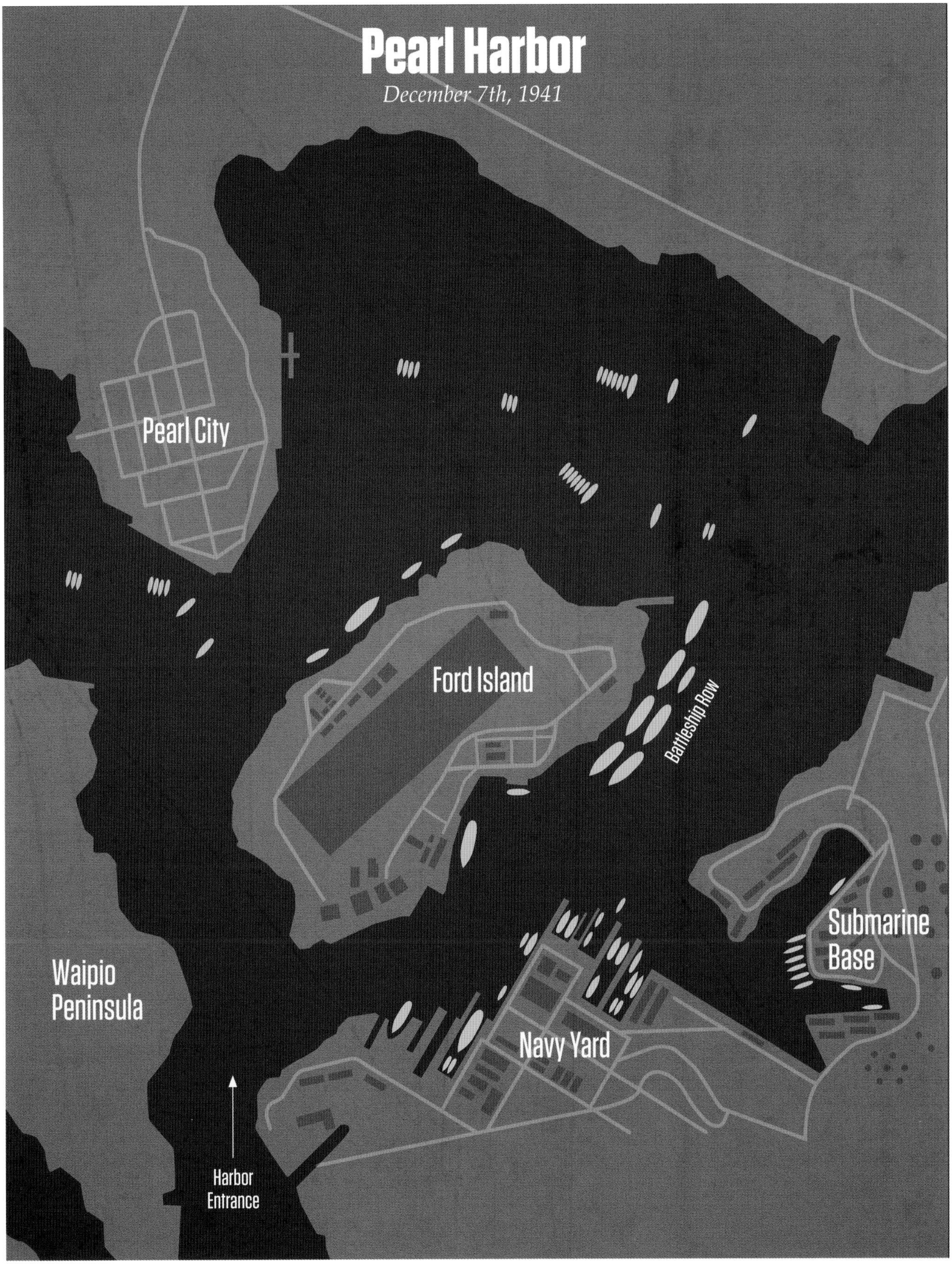

Pearl Harbor
December 7th, 1941

Pearl City

Ford Island

Battleship Row

Waipio
Peninsula

Navy Yard

Submarine
Base

Harbor
Entrance

Pacific Fleet

Aircraft Carriers x 3

Battleships x 9

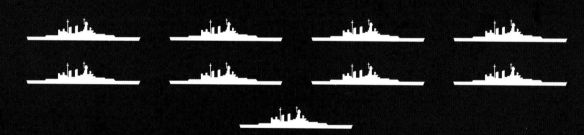

The U.S. fleet stationed at Pearl Harbor was known as the Pacific Fleet. By December 1941, this group of vessels included nine battleships: the *Arizona, Pennsylvania, Utah, Maryland, Oklahoma, Tennessee, West Virginia, Nevada,* and *California*. Battleships were the most powerful vessels in the fleet. They were fitted with thick steel armor and powerful guns. A single ship carried a crew of 1,300 to 2,300 men. Each had everything from doctor's offices to print shops and post offices. The Pacific Fleet also included 3 aircraft carriers, 21 **cruisers**, 53 destroyers, and 23 submarines.

Cruisers x21

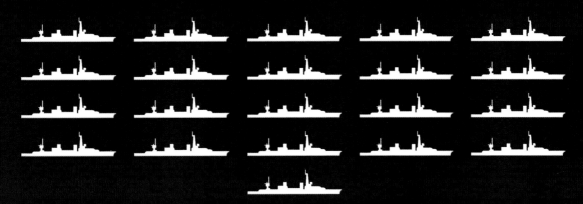

Destroyers x53

Submarines x23

The largest aircraft carriers used in World War II could hold up to 100 airplanes.

U.S. officials thought keeping the fleet at Pearl Harbor would prevent Japan from attacking. But many in Japan saw the Pacific Fleet at Pearl Harbor as a threat. Japanese commander Admiral Isoroku Yamamoto called it a "dagger pointed at our throat." American and Japanese **diplomats** held talks. The U.S. demanded that Japan remove its forces from Asia. Japan refused.

The two sides failed to reach an agreement. American officials began to expect a Japanese attack. They thought the attack would occur in the Pacific. But few believed it would be at Pearl Harbor. The base was 3,400 miles (5,472 km) from Japan. Closer targets such as Thailand, the Philippines, or Borneo seemed more likely.

WAR EXERCISE

A 1932 joint U.S. Army-Navy war exercise pitted two teams against each other. One team defended Pearl Harbor. The other attacked. The offensive team launched a surprise air attack from aircraft carriers. The attack occurred on a Sunday morning. The planes dropped fake bombs on the island's airfields and ships. The attack was a success. But navy officials said it could never happen in real life. Japanese naval leaders took note.

MOBILIZING FORCES

Admiral Yamamoto knew Japan couldn't win a long-term war against the U.S. But he thought if Japan struck first, the U.S. would be weakened. He believed U.S. forces would quickly give up. He planned a sneak attack.

A Japanese spy in Hawaii watched the U.S. Pacific Fleet's movements. He told Japanese leaders what he observed. Half the Pacific Fleet went to sea for **maneuvers** on Monday. They returned on Wednesday. The other half of the fleet left on Thursday. They came back on Saturday. The entire fleet stayed in the harbor on Sunday. Japanese officials decided to attack on a Sunday.

In September 1941, Japanese pilots began training for a new mission. They were not told their target. But they practiced flying low over water. They worked on dropping torpedoes on battleship-sized targets. The

ADMIRAL YAMAMOTO

"We trained fiercely, morning, noon, and night. We never had a day off, except when it rained. And we knew that we were about to start a war with America. We were shown drawings of ships on large cards and told to learn them. Two of them were the Pennsylvania *and the* Oklahoma.*"*

- Yuji Akamatsu, Japanese pilot, on training for Pearl Harbor

Japanese military tweaked its torpedoes, too. Standard torpedoes traveled 100 feet (30.5 m) underwater before exploding. But Pearl Harbor's waters were only 40 feet (12.2 m) deep. The Japanese added wooden fins to their torpedoes. This kept them from dropping too deep. It made them a perfect weapon for the shallow harbor.

On November 17, 1941, the Japanese fleet set sail for the Kuril Islands. These islands are northeast of Japan. Once they arrived, the Japanese sailors and pilots

Japanese officials kept their target secret from most of their military, including fighter pilots, until shortly before the attack.

learned their mission. They spent three more days training. Sailors studied scale models of the harbor. Some wrote goodbye letters to their families.

By November 26, the Japanese strike force was sailing southeast toward Hawaii.

It included 6 aircraft carriers, 2 battleships, 3 cruisers, 9 destroyers, 8 oilers, and 30 submarines. In order to succeed, the mission had to remain a secret. So the ships did not communicate over the radio. They maintained blackouts, keeping all light sources

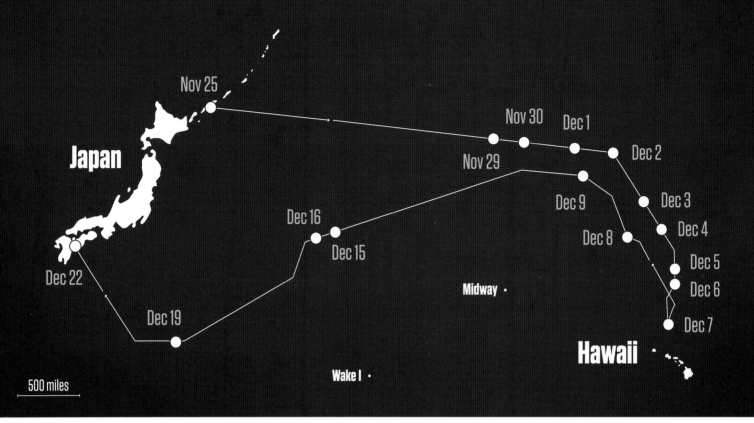

Route of Japanese carrier task force

Nov 25

Japan

Nov 30 Dec 1

Nov 29 Dec 2

Dec 16 Dec 9 Dec 3

Dec 15 Dec 4

Dec 8 Dec 5

Dec 22 Dec 6

Midway ·

Dec 19 Dec 7

Hawaii ·

500 miles

Wake I ·

hidden. And they did not throw any trash overboard.

Their tactics worked. Officials in Washington, D.C., knew the Japanese fleet had moved. But they didn't know where it had gone. On November 27, the U.S. Pacific Fleet received a war warning from naval command. It said that Japan's aircraft carrier groups could not be located. Some feared Japan might be about to attack. The warning urged commanders to make preparations. It also said not to alarm local citizens. Even so, a headline in the *Honolulu Adver-*

tiser on November 30 read, "Japanese May Strike Over Weekend!" But the weekend came and went without an attack. Many people relaxed.

The next weekend, crews at Pearl Harbor prepared for an upcoming inspection. They removed ammunition from around their ships' **antiaircraft** guns. They stored it in locked compartments below deck. On some ships, sailors opened the watertight hatches to air them out. These hatches were made to keep a ship from flooding if its hull was damaged. At the island's airfields,

The Yamashiro was among the 12 battleships in the fleet of the Imperial Japanese Navy during World War II.

When not on duty, naval personnel had time to relax; some played instruments, while others enjoyed sports and other activities.

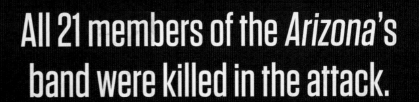

All 21 members of the *Arizona's* band were killed in the attack.

pilots removed ammunition from planes. They feared that Japanese American islanders might sabotage the planes.

The night of December 6, many sailors enjoyed time off. Some listened to a contest of the fleet's bands. Others went to the movies. Some ate dinner in Honolulu. Then they returned to the harbor. The fleet's three aircraft carriers were at sea. But most of the Pacific Fleet was in the harbor. Six battleships were moored along what sailors called Battleship Row. They lined the eastern side of Ford Island. This is a narrow strip of land in the middle of the harbor. The other three battleships were stationed nearby.

That night, Lieutenant General Walter C. Short looked toward Pearl Harbor. He saw the lights shining from the deck of each battleship. And he worried about what a good target they made.

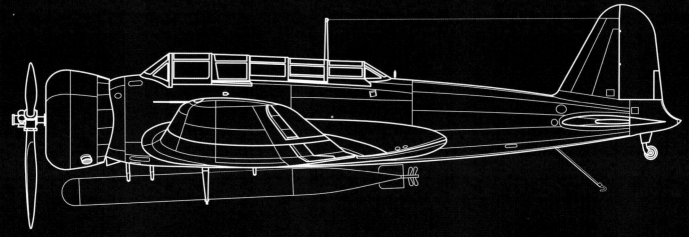

Nakajima B5N (Kate)

crew - 3 (pilot, commander, gunner)
loaded weight - 8,380 pounds (3,801 kg)
top speed - 235 miles (378 km) per hour

KATES, VALS, AND ZEROS

Allied forces gave code names to the Japanese aircraft used during World War II. The planes used at Pearl Harbor included 171 Kates, 108 Vals, and 135 Zeros. Kates were bombers. They carried torpedoes and armor-piercing bombs. Vals were dive-bombers. They dove in close to the water. Then they dropped smaller bombs. Zeros were fighter planes. They could make quick turns. They were armed with machine guns and cannons.

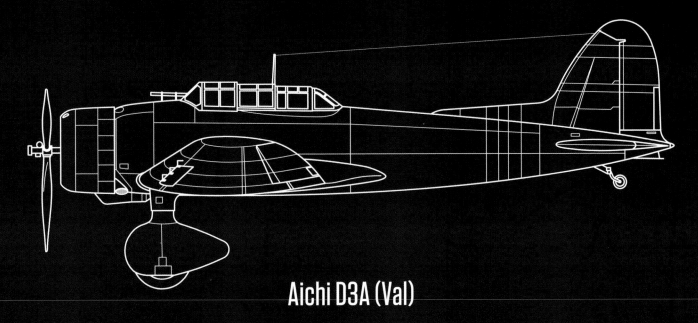

Aichi D3A (Val)

crew - 2 (pilot, gunner)
loaded weight - 5,309 pounds (2,408 kg)
top speed - 242 miles (389 km) per hour

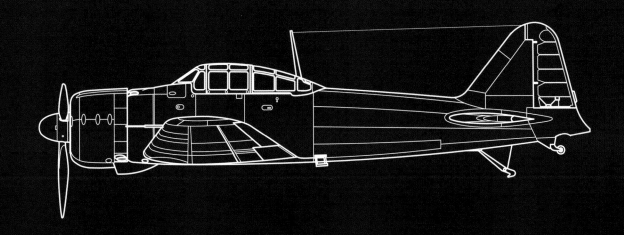

Mitsubishi A6M (Zero)

crew - 1 (pilot)
loaded weight - 3,704 pounds (1,680 kg)
top speed - 332 miles (534 km) per hour

III

NOT A DRILL

The Japanese planned to launch their attack from 230 miles (370 km) north of Oahu. The strike force reached the launch point before sunrise on Sunday, December 7, 1941. At 6:00 A.M., 183 Japanese planes took off from the decks of the aircraft carriers. Japanese submarines also made their way toward the harbor. The submarines carried five midget subs. The midget subs were battery-powered. They were designed to sneak into the harbor to fire torpedoes.

Around 6:45 A.M., the U.S. destroyer *Ward* sank one of the midget subs just outside the harbor. About 15 minutes later, 2 soldiers at a **radar** station noticed something odd. Numerous blips had suddenly appeared on their monitor. These blips indicated planes moving toward the island. The planes were about 132 miles (212 km) away. The soldiers reported what they

Japanese aircraft carriers brought warplanes within fighting distance of Hawaii.

The line of ships anchored at Pearl Harbor was known as Battleship Row—and it made the perfect target.

saw. They were told not to worry. The blips were likely American bomber planes. The bombers were supposed to land on the island that day.

Meanwhile, in Washington, D.C., officials discovered a coded Japanese message. The message told Japanese diplomats to end their peace talks at 1:00 P.M. Eastern time. That was 7:30 A.M. in the Pacific. Many U.S. officials believed the message meant Japan planned to attack. But they still didn't know where. They sent a message to all U.S. bases in the Pacific. The message arrived in Oahu around 7:40 A.M. But it was not marked urgent. Commanders at Pearl Harbor didn't see it.

At 7:49 A.M., the Japanese planes reached Pearl Harbor. Air commander Captain Mitsuo Fuchida gave the signal to attack. Some of the planes fired on army, navy, and marine airfields on Oahu. Other planes went into a steep dive over the harbor. They leveled off at 25 feet (7.6 m) above the water. Then

"Sunday morning, I was standing looking out at this very peaceful scene of the hangar line, and suddenly this airplane dove out of the sky, dropped an object which exploded into a huge orange blossom, and then pulled up sharply.... I ... strapped a ... pistol around my pajamas and ran down to the flight line."

- Phil Rasmussen, U.S. Army pilot, Wheeler Field

they released torpedoes. Each torpedo carried 450 pounds (204 kg) of explosives. Other planes remained higher. They dropped bombs that punched through the ships' deck armor.

Within moments, black smoke billowed from several ships. The *Utah*, *Oklahoma*, *West Virginia*, *Nevada*, and *California* were all hit. Many of the fleet's smaller ships were hit as well. At 7:58 A.M., an alarm went out: "Air raid, Pearl Harbor. This is not a drill!" Men aboard the ships raced for their battle stations. Some fired antiaircraft guns at the Japanese planes.

But the attack continued. At 8:06 A.M., a 1,760-pound (798 kg) bomb smashed into the *Arizona*. It ignited a powder **magazine** at the front of the ship. A huge explosion rocked the vessel. More than 1,000 men died instantly.

Minutes later, the damaged *Utah* and *Oklahoma* rolled over. Their open hatches had filled with water. Men were trapped inside both ships. As bombs continued to fall, sailors worked to reach the trapped men. Others cruised the harbor in small

THE ATTACK ON PEARL HARBOR

On December 6, the Arizona *had taken on nearly 1.5 million gallons (5.7 million l) of fuel, which fed the fires.*

USS Arizona

"With all these fumes and stuff, my eyes were burning.
I had salt water, gasoline, bunker oil, and stuff all in
my eyes; and I'd swallowed I don't know how much
salt water.... We stayed in that compartment rapping
out this SOS. I don't know how long it was."

Garlen Eslick, U.S. Navy seaman, on being trapped aboard the USS Oklahoma

Large antiaircraft guns on naval vessels did not exist prior to 1940 but became standard during the war.

boats. They pulled the injured from the water. They had to dodge oil fires spreading across the water's surface. Finally, at 8:35 A.M., the attack ended.

Twenty minutes later, a second wave of Japanese planes buzzed the island. This time, the American response was stronger. Antiaircraft missiles peppered the air. But many of the missiles missed their targets. Some landed in Honolulu, killing civilians. More American ships took hits. Among them was the *Pennsylvania*. Finally, around 10:00 A.M., the Japanese planes flew off. They didn't return.

The Japanese attack had lasted little more than two hours. In that time, it had damaged or destroyed 19 American ships. Nearly 160 planes had also been destroyed. Another 170 planes were badly damaged. A total of 2,403 Americans had died. Another 1,178 were injured. Japan had lost only 29 aircraft, 5 midget submarines, and 129 men.

The attack at Pearl Harbor left hundreds of U.S. military aircraft damaged or destroyed.

ATTACK ON PEARL HARBOR
Timeline

3:00 A.M. A decoded message hinting at Japanese action is delivered to President Roosevelt.

3:42 A.M. A patrolling minesweeper spots a submarine outside the entrance to Pearl Harbor.

6:00 A.M. Japanese planes take off from aircraft carriers on a choppy sea.

7:02 A.M. A radar station on Oahu reports 50 or more aircraft are headed toward the island.

7:49 A.M. Japanese air commander Mitsuo Fuchida gives the attack order.

8:06 A.M. The *Arizona* is struck and sinks within minutes.

8:35 A.M. The first wave of Japanese aircraft breaks off its attack.

8:55 A.M. The Japanese return with a second wave, meeting heavy antiaircraft fire.

10:00 A.M. Japanese planes return to their carriers north of Oahu.

INFAMOUS DATE

President Roosevelt learned of the attack 10 minutes after it began. By afternoon, radio stations had spread the news. People across the country showed their patriotism. Many communities held **vigils**. Those who had once been against war now supported it. Young men rushed to sign up for military service.

On December 8, President Roosevelt addressed Congress. He called December 7, 1941, "a date which will live in **infamy**." Congress declared war on Japan. Within three days, the U.S. was also at war with the other Axis nations, Germany and Italy.

At first, Japan dominated battles in the Pacific. Japanese forces invaded the Philippines, Guam, Wake Island, Thailand, and Hong Kong. The Pacific Fleet had suffered many losses. But sailors at Pearl Harbor worked to rebuild the ships damaged in the attack.

President Roosevelt asked Congress to affirm that the attack constituted "a state of war" between the U.S. and Japan.

WHOSE FAULT?

Investigations have blamed various people for the attack on Pearl Harbor. Days after the attack, Lieutenant General Walter C. Short (pictured) and Admiral Husband E. Kimmel were removed from their posts. A January 1942 report accused both of failing in their duties. A 1944 report blamed officials in Washington, D.C. A 1995 report shared blame among government officials and military commanders. This report cited a lack of communication and preparation.

The 1976 film *Midway* dramatized the events of the World War II Battle of Midway in the Pacific.

Within weeks, the *Pennsylvania*, *Tennessee*, and *Maryland* were ready for service. The *West Virginia*, *Nevada*, and *California* were also eventually repaired. The *Arizona*, *Oklahoma*, and *Utah* could not be saved. But divers recovered guns and other equipment from them.

In June 1942, many of the repaired ships took part in the Battle of Midway. Four of the six Japanese aircraft carriers from the Pearl Harbor attack were sunk in the battle. (The other two carriers were sunk in battle in 1944.) The American victory at Midway marked a turning point in the war. Afterward, Japan suffered a series of defeats.

Meanwhile, in the U.S., many people

Many of the Japanese Americans sent to the camps were children, whose clothing was tagged with their family's identification number.

became distrustful of Japanese Americans. Many Japanese Americans lived on the West Coast. Some people feared they would serve as spies for Japan. The U.S. government set up 10 **internment** camps. More than 100,000 Japanese Americans were forced to leave their homes and live in these camps. Conditions in the camps were often terrible. They were located in isolated deserts. They were surrounded by barbed wire and guards. Families had to cram into tiny rooms. They slept on sacks filled with straw. Sickness spread quickly in the close quarters. Prisoners had to remain in the camps for nearly three years. By the time they could leave, many had lost their homes and businesses.

On August 6, 1945, the U.S. dropped an

8.9.1945

Atomic bomb dropped on Nagasaki

atomic bomb on Hiroshima, Japan. Three days later, it dropped another bomb on Nagasaki. Japan surrendered. World War II was over. (The war in Europe had ended with German surrender in May.)

Americans didn't forget about Pearl Harbor after the war. People around the country continue to honor December 7 as Pearl Harbor Remembrance Day. In 1962, the USS *Arizona* Memorial opened. The 184-foot-long (56.1 m) memorial spans the

sunken *Arizona*. The top of the ship is visible below the murky water. Oil continues to leak from the ship. Drops of oil collect on the surface of the water. Some people call them "black tears," or the "tears of the *Arizona*." A marble wall inside the memorial lists the names of all 1,177 men killed aboard the ship.

In 2016, Japanese prime minister Shinzo Abe visited the memorial. He and U.S. president Barack Obama dropped flowers

As the second atomic bomb, "Fat Man," was detonated over Nagasaki, it created a mushroom cloud in the atmosphere.

"To forget Pearl Harbor is to forget the good and evil
 that human beings are capable of in times of crisis.
 Without a vivid memory of this event, we may lack
 the fortitude and the preparedness to withstand future
 assaults on our country and its democratic ideals."

Senator Daniel K. Inouye, who lived in Hawaii at the time of the attack

The joint visit of Shinzo Abe and Barack Obama in 2016 hearkened to a spirit of reconciliation between the two nations.

into the water. Abe offered his sympathy for those who had died. President Obama said Abe's visit "reminds us that wars can end." He noted that Japan and the U.S. were once enemies. But they have become strong allies.

Today, more than 1.5 million people visit the *Arizona* each year. They watch the oil rise from the ship. They read the names of those who died. More than 75 years after the attack, they remember the day that lives in infamy.

GLOSSARY

antiaircraft weapons designed to fire into the air to attack aircraft

cruisers medium-sized, fast warships with less armor and firepower than battleships

destroyer a small, fast warship armed with guns, torpedoes, and missiles

diplomats people chosen by their government to represent their country in dealings with the governments of other countries

Great Depression the period from 1929 to 1939, when the U.S. experienced the collapse of banks and businesses, causing widespread unemployment and homelessness

infamy famed for something bad or negative

internment imprisonment or confinement, often during war

magazine the location in a ship for storing ammunition and explosives

maneuvers practice movements carried out by sailors, pilots, or soldiers in preparation for battle

radar a system that uses radio waves to determine the speed and position of an object

torpedoes long, narrow projectiles launched by a ship, submarine, or airplane at an enemy ship

vigils quiet gatherings, often at night and often to mark someone's death

READ MORE

Bowman, Chris. *The Attack on Pearl Harbor.* Minneapolis: Bellwether Media, 2015.

Gallagher, Michael. *Decisive Battles.* Mankato, Minn.: Sea-to-Sea, 2009.

WEBSITES

National Geographic: Remembering Pearl Harbor
http://www.nationalgeographic.com/pearlharbor/

View photos and maps of Pearl Harbor, and read survivors' stories.

National Park Service: World War II Valor in the Pacific
https://www.nps.gov/valr/index.htm

Learn more about the ships stationed at Pearl Harbor, the attack, and the USS *Arizona* Memorial.

Note: Every effort has been made to ensure that any websites listed above were active at the time of publication. However, because of the nature of the Internet, it is impossible to guarantee that these sites will remain active indefinitely or that their contents will not be altered.

INDEX